T0066270

# *Wolfgang Amadeus*
# MOZART

# CONCERTO
*in*
## A MAJOR
*for*
## CLARINET
*and*
## ORCHESTRA

To access audio visit:
**www.halleonard.com/mylibrary**

Enter Code
6955-0214-1279-8311

ISBN 978-1-59615-265-6

 Music Minus One

EXCLUSIVELY DISTRIBUTED BY
**HAL•LEONARD®**
7777 W. BLUEMOUND RD. P.O. BOX 13819 MILWAUKEE, WI 53213

© 2007 MMO Music Group, Inc.
All Rights Reserved

For all works contained herein:
Unauthorized copying, arranging, adapting, recording, Internet posting, public performance,
or other distribution of the printed or recorded music in this publication is an infringement of copyright.
Infringers are liable under the law.

Visit Hal Leonard Online at
**www.halleonard.com**

Music Minus One

3238

# CONTENTS

## A NOTE ON THE RE-PITCHED VERSION

WHILE THIS CONCERTO was originally intended for the Clarinet in A, and it is therefore desirable to perform it on that instrument, it may be played on the B-flat clarinet with proper transposition. We have included a second engraving of the quintet transposed for execution on the B-flat clarinet while maintaining the A-major key of the original piece.

For this MMO edition, however, we have also added a second version of the concerto, transposed to B-flat major, for those who don't possess an A clarinet and who find the key-transposition for B-flat clarinet too difficult to play. To play this alternative B-flat-major version, perform on your B-flat clarinet while reading the version for *Clarinet in A.*

## MOZART'S CLARINET CONCERTO IN A MAJOR, KV622

ONE WOULD BE HARD PUT to find a more satisfying piece of music than Mozart's Clarinet Concerto in A major. Its transcendent, golden beauty is as warm and touching as music is capable of being without an overt digging at our heartstrings. And, indeed, its beauty is matched by its simplicity. Here Mozart displays that most deceptive and difficult artistic feat, one that most lesser artists endlessly fail to achieve: that "less is more." A lasting work of art does not entail showing off one's talents, but rather capturing a subject's psychological essence—its honesty—in as clear and simple a statement as possible. Mozart proves this again and again in so many of his compositions, and we are eternally surprised at his straightforwardness and lack of embellishment. And it is in this, his last concerto (completed in October 1791, a mere two months before his death), that Mozart's "art of simplicity" possibly finds its finest expression.

✂ ✂

The first marked exposure Wolfgang Amadeus Mozart (1756-1791) had to the clarinet—his era's newest addition to the woodwind family—took place when the young composer was visiting Mannheim with his mother in 1777-8. Mozart had written for the instrument as early as 1771, but it wasn't until Mannheim that he really began to discover the potential riches that lay in the instrument. In the performances he heard, he was impressed and inspired by this instrument's warm tones and wide-ranging *timbre*. But his creative impulses regarding this new instrument weren't allowed immediate expression: at that time it was still considered an unusual instrument, and virtuosic players were a rarity.

Only toward the end of Mozart's life did the clarinet become—in Austria and in Vienna in particular—a more familiarly accepted member of woodwind sections in orchestras, and it was only then that Mozart composed specifically for the instrument. It is appropriate that Mozart's final flowering as a composer, just shortly before his death, coincides with his composing for an instrument in which he found so much sympathy with his own musical sensibility.

The intensity of Mozart's love of the clarinet is evident in the brilliance of some of his compositions for this instrument—the Trio for Clarinet, Viola and Piano in E-flat major, KV498 (1786), the Clarinet Quintet in A major, KV581 (1789), the *obbligati* in two of the arias in *La clemenza di Tito* (1791)—but it is most clearly displayed in his Clarinet Concerto in A major, KV622 (1791). It is no coincidence that Mozart composed all of these works for his friend Anton Stadler (1753-1812)—for here was a clarinetist of greater virtuosity than any person known at that time.

When confronted with brilliance approaching his own, Mozart's inspiration knew no bounds; with Stadler in mind, his imagination soared high. This was despite the dislike members of Mozart's family held for Stadler due to his "distasteful" personal qualities: Stadler shared with Mozart not only Freemasonry but a love of gambling. Other accounts of Stadler indicate he was quite irresponsible. On more than a few occasions it seems Mozart loaned Stadler substantial sums of money that Stadler never paid back. Mozart didn't mind, however; not only did he enjoy the man's company, he respected Stadler's genius as a clarinetist. Mozart, like so many genuine artists, excused much in his fellow man if that fellow possessed a measure of the artistry he himself possessed.

What is it that the clarinet can do that so obviously affected Mozart? Most likely the answer is in this instrument's ability to mimic the range and emotions produced by the human voice. Mozart undoubtedly noted the clarinet's ability to sing with a warmth of feeling not unlike that produced by the greatest of singers, thus enabling him to compose music which, though conceived on a more intimate scale, touched a deeply human chord. It is no coincidence that written records of Stadler's playing stress his ability to capture through his playing a uniquely human tone.

Stadler was fascinated by the deep notes of his clarinet, and to further the low range, he designed, in collaboration with the local Viennese clarinetist and instrument maker Theodor Lotz, a clarinet with an extension that could play down to a written C. This was two octaves below a middle C, which is two tones lower than normally possible. It was for this "basset clarinet" (as it is generally called today; Stadler gave it no special name) that Mozart wrote this concerto. But as wonderful and rich as Stadler's basset clarinet must have sounded, it did not catch on.

Unfortunately, Mozart's original 1791 autograph score for the concerto has been lost. The earliest sources are three printed editions from 1799 to 1801, almost ten years after Mozart's death, and in each of these the Concerto has been restructured to accommodate the range of the ordinary clarinet in A. There is no evidence that Mozart did this himself; in any event this would have been most unlikely, as he became increasingly ill after its composition.

It comes as a surprise to many that the accepted score to this concerto, certainly the most beloved ever written for clarinet as well as the greatest of Mozart's wind concerti, was actually re-arranged by an unknown person. But despite its being in a slightly inauthentic condition, its status remains undiminished. Fortunately in 1802, a reviewer of one of the re-arranged published versions, who was quite familiar with Mozart's original version, noted many of the differences; this has been instrumental in recent reconstructed versions of the Concerto for the basset clarinet.

It is also ironic that Mozart first began composing the Concerto (possibly as early as 1789) not in A major, but in G major, and not for the clarinet but for the basset horn. 199 measures of the first movement of this false-start survive (as KV584b or 621b) and they are virtually identical to the concerto as we now know it. Why Mozart ultimately chose to write it for Stadler's extended clarinet is a mystery. We can only be grateful that he did.

The final irony regarding the concerto is its lack of opportunity for cadenzas. One would assume that Mozart would allow room for these since he had composed the piece not only for a friend but for a virtuoso clarinetist. But we must assume that Mozart, in all of his musical wisdom, sensed the completeness of the piece without cadenzas. Throughout, the clarinet's registers are fully exploited without it losing its integration with the orchestra. If virtuoso exhibition is sacrificed, it is for reasons of greater unity and simplicity—both of which Mozart achieved magnificently.

—*Douglas Scharmann*

# CONCERTO

IN A MAJOR

FOR

CLARINET

AND

ORCHESTRA

KV622

BY

# WOLFGANG AMADEUS MOZART

## SOLO CLARINET IN B-FLAT

# CONCERTO
## for Clarinet and Orchestra
## in A Major

### Solo B-flat Clarinet

Wofgang Amadeus Mozart
KV622

Solo B - Flat Clarinet

12

Solo B - Flat Clarinet

MMO 3238

# II.

CADENZA

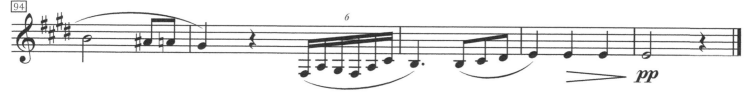

# III. Rondo

*4 taps (2 measures) precede orchestra*
*Start on upbeat of 4th tap.*

# CONCERTO

IN A MAJOR

FOR

CLARINET

AND

ORCHESTRA

KV622

BY

# WOLFGANG

# AMADEUS

# MOZART

SOLO CLARINET IN A

MMO 3238

# CONCERTO
## for Clarinet and Orchestra
## in A Major

### Solo A Clarinet

Wofgang Amadeus Mozart
KV622

Solo A Clarinet

Solo A Clarinet

# II.

34

Solo A Clarinet

# III. Rondo

4 taps (2 measures) precede orchestra
*Start on upbeat of 4 th tap.*

Solo A Clarinet

MMO 3238

Solo A Clarinet

Solo A Clarinet

Engraving: Wieslaw Novak

MMO 3238

# Mozart

## Clarinet Concerto in A major, KV622

*Wolfgang Amadeus Mozart (1756-1791)*

One of the great pinnacles of musical composition came with the release in the early 19th century of the Clarinet Concerto, which Mozart composed in the last months of his life for his friend Anton Stadler. Interestingly, it was written for Stadler's own "improved" extra-long clarinet, which encompassed an extra several notes on the low end of the clarinet's usual range. Stadler's clarinet never caught on, and for publication—ten years after Mozart's death—the concerto was slightly modified to suit the standard clarinet; it is this version which has been passed down to us (the original Stadler version remains lost).

Mozart did not make extensive use of the clarinet until comparatively late in his career, but he wrote exquisitely for the instrument, and the two scores dedicated to Stadler—the Quintet, KV581 and the Concerto, KV622—are among his most beautiful works. The Clarinet Concerto is in the conventional three movements, with music that transcends conventionality in its remarkable sense of repose and serenity, and what Bernhard Paumgartner has called "its incredible warmth of tone, perfect balance and unmatched perfection of style."

The concerto's popularity has held to this day. Its famous slow movement was featured in the 1985 Academy-Award-winning motion picture *Out of Africa,* which again brought it to the forefront of attention of the general public. Long a favorite with both audiences and performers, its gentle, soulful qualities and charmingly playful melodies combine with a chamber-like orchestration for a delightful and rewarding experience for every clarinetist. MMO is pleased to make this ever-popular treasure available in a new digital recording which you will enjoy for years to come.